GAUDI

Text, photographs, design, lay-out and printing, entirely created by the technical department of EDITORIAL ESCUDO DE ORO, S.A.

Rights of total or partial reproduction and translation reserved.

6th Edition

I.S.B.N. 84-378-1632-7

Dep. Legal B. 34568-1999

Editorial Escudo de Oro, S.A.

(Photograph by Branguli).

Close-up of the waterfall in the Ciutadela.

AN ARCHITECT OF GENIUS

Antonio Gaudí Cornet, born in Reus, Spain, on June 25th, 1852, is with justice considered to be one of the greatest architects of the last two centuries. He came from a family of humble social status: his father, grandfather and great-grandfather had been coppersmiths. Gaudí received his secondary education at the Piarist school in Reus and in 1870 he entered the School of Architecture in Barcelona.

This was a man of impassioned temperament, gifted with exceptional intelligence. These characteristics, in conjunction with his having been born in Reus in a family of coppersmiths, had a decisive influence on both his life and his work. As Salvador Tarragó, the architect, wrote, Gaudí «always considered his descent from pot- and kettle-making men fundamental, and frequently asserted that it was the main cause of his seeing forms directly in space and solving his problems in it, without needing the help of graphic representation in plans.»

From 1876 to 1878 Gaudí worked on diverse projects with the architects

Villar, Sala and Martorell, as also with the master builder Fontseré. He finished his degree in architecture on January 4th, 1878, obtained his qualifications as an architect on March 15th, and opened an office in Calle Call, Barcelona. In the same year he sent the plan for the Mataró Co-operative to Paris, where the International Exhibition was being held. In 1883 Gaudí travelled to Banyuls, Elne and Carcassonne; he also undertook the plans for the Sagrada Familia (Holy Family) Cathedral in Barcelona. Between 1890 and 1894 he travelled to Andalusia, León and Astorga; he was to leave profound architectural influences on the latter cities.

Gaudí was awarded the First Prize of Barcelona *Ayuntamiento* (City Hall), for the Casa Calvet, on September 3rd, 1901.

He was in Palma de Mallorca in 1904, and returned there in 1914. In 1910 Gaudí achieved great success with his exhibition at the Société Générale des Beaux Arts in Paris. He fell seriously ill the following year, having contracted Malta fever, and was given the viaticum in Puigcerdá.

The architect dedicated the whole of 1914 exclusively to work on his ambitious plan for the Sagrada Familia.

Gaudí was knocked down by a tram on June 7th, 1926, and died in Barcelona three days later.

One of Gaudí's street lamps in the Plaça Reial.

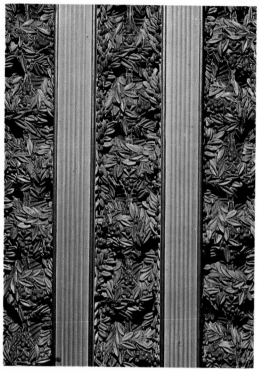

Three details of the decorations of the Casa Vicens.

MONUMENTS BY GAUDÍ

Since Gaudí's death the esteem enjoyed by his architectural oeuvre has attained universality. The great Catalan architect designed many buildings that are considered nothing less than masterpieces: buildings as diverse as Casa Vicens, decorated with singular charm and imagination (located in Calle Carolinas, in the popular Gracia quarter of Barcelona), the edifices in Park Güell, the Sagrada Familia, Palacio Güell, La Pedrera and the Bishops' Palace in Astorga.

Part of the Casa Vicens. ▷

Door to the garden from the small smoking-room and two details of the decoration of the dining-room of the Casa Vicens in the Carrer Carolines.

Entrance to the house built for Máximo Diaz de Quijano, popularly known as "El Capricho", in Comillas (Santander).

Gate and stables of the Pabellones Güell.

Fragment of the gate of the Pabellones Güell. ▷

The Sagrada Familia (Holy Family) Cathedral in Barcelona is unquestionably the greatest of Gaudí's monuments.

This is one of his most famous buildings; he began work on it in 1884 and left it unfinished on his death in 1926.

The crypt, apse and Nativity Façade were built under Gaudí's supervision. The construction of the Passion Façade commenced in 1952, under the super-

General view of the Colegio Teresiano.

Wrought iron gate of the Colegio Teresiano.

vision of his colleagues Domènec Sugrañes, Francesc Quintana and Isidre Puig i Boada.

Gaudí said of the Sagrada Familia that it was not the last cathedral, rather, the first of a new series. The brilliant architect dedicated a considerable part of his life to raising this expiatory church. The Nativity Façade, with the distinctive silhouettes of its four spires, is the most appreciated part of his work: it displays a wealth of ornamentation, with statues depicting the Nativity and other scenes of the life of Christ. The spires designed by Gaudí constitute one of the most widely popularized images of Barcelona abroad; they are helicoidal in shape, with spiral staircases. This is the last work executed by the architect. The Sagrada Familia spires are 100 m

A facet of the Palau Güell (Theatre Museum).

high and dominate the panorama of Barcelona to this day, although buildings of considerable height have been raised in the city. The cathedral is one of the obligatory sights for the many thousands of tourists who visit Barcelona every year.

The church was intended to become a centre for the promotion of the Catholic faith; and the Asociación Espiritual de Devotos de San José (Spiritual Association devoted to S Joseph), the owner of the Sagrada Familia, was given special assistance from the outset by Leo XIII, in the form of indulgences, blessings and even the return of half of the funds collected throughout the world by the Association each year and paid to the Vatican, so as to speed work on the expiatory church.

In 1900 Joan Maragall, the poet, defined the Sagrada Familia as "the Cathedral of the poor"; in 1905 it became the "Nova Catedral" of "Gran Barcelona."

The doorway called Puerta de la Esperanza is on the left of the Nativity Façade, it is crowned by the Virgin Mary's anagram and decorated with scenes relating to the Holy Family. A stone from the mountain of Montserrat appears in the upper part of this "Door of Hope."

The Puerta de la Caridad stands at the centre of the façade; it is decorated with abundant carvings of plants — a symbolical hymn of love for the Supreme Creator. The "Door of Charity" is adorned with various scenes alluding to the life of the Virgin Mary, and Jesus' genealogical tree is depicted on its mullion.

Gates of the Palau Güell (Carrer Nou de la Rambla).

View of the roof of the Palau Güell from the Carrer Nou de la Rambla.

Dome of the vestibule with the windows of the bedroom floor below. ▷

Staircase and
liturgic lamp,
20th century.
Mallorca Cathedral.

Mallorca Cathedral.
Canopy - Bell tower. ▷

The Bishops' Palace in Astorga is another outstanding creation of the Catalan genius.

Gaudí was commissioned to build this Palace by his friend Bishop Don Juan Bautista Grau Vallespinós, who was also a native of Reus; the construction began in 1887 and was interrupted on the prelate's death in 1894. The building is only partly the work of Gaudí: it was completed in 1915 by Guereta, who did not follow the original design.

The Palace now houses the Museum of the Pilgrims' Road to Santiago.

Casa de Botines, located in León, also merits special mention.

This large mansion, standing in the centre of León, was built by Gaudí from 1891 to 1894. He was commissioned by Señores Fernández and Andrés, textile merchants in this provincial capital. The architect from Reus devoted the ground floor and basement to a store for textiles, the main floor to the owners' residence, and the other storeys of the building to flats for tenants.

The sober lines characterising Casa de Botines — built of stone — constitute an image of robust originality within the general urban appearance of the city. The main front has turrets at the corners and displays interesting grilles.

This singular edifice stands in the Plaza de San Marcelo; it is one of León's main tourist attractions.

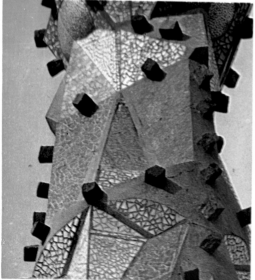

The famous towers of the church of the Sagrada Familia.

Detail of the sculptural group symbolising the Massacre of the Innocents.

The fascinating design of Casa de Figueras should be highlighted within Gaudí's architecture.

Also known as Bellesguard, this house was built by Gaudí from 1900 to 1902; it is located on the slopes of El Tibidabo, from whence there is an extensive, beautiful panorama of Barcelona stretching from the mountains to the sea. This privileged site was previously occupied by a country mansion built by King Martín I, "the Humane."

Gaudí used the vestiges of the royal mansion in the construction of the property's entrance lodge. Casa de Figueras is a small, elegant building, harmoniously integrated into the splendid landscape of El Tibidabo. The stones of the mansion, in shades of green and grey, come from the site where it stands and are well matched with the green colour predominating in the surrounding area.

In the interior, the house displays ceilings combining brick arches and vaults: the shape of the roof is different in each room. The one in the attic is the most interesting, the experts consider it to be "one of the most successful spaces" in Gaudí's brilliant oeuvre. The serried spears of wrought iron at the entrance to the property, the fine stair-well by which one enters the mansion, and the grilles of the ground-floor windows (also wrought iron) are all very interesting.

In short, Casa de Figueras is one of Gaudí's architectural gems.

The Holy Family group (sculpture by J. Busquets).

Tops of the bell towers of the Passion
Facade built by Gaudí's successors.

Various parts of the Sagrada Familia. ▷

The Charity Gate on the Nativity Facade represents a large cypress (the church) where birds (the faithful) flock.

Twisted shapes on the spires.

Inside a bell tower. ▷

The staircase of the towers on the
Nativity Facade of the Sagrada Familia.

The Passion Facade as it is today.

Sculptures Josep M. Subirachs.

The facade of the Bishop's Palace in Astorga.

Casa Calvet is one of Gaudí's most interesting civil monuments.

This building, characteristic of his work, was constructed from 1898 to 1904. It is a typical middle-class house of the Barcelona of the Ensanche ("expan-sion" of that period), built for Don Pedro M. Calvet, a textile manufacturer from this city.

Gaudí's unmistakable architectural style is visible in the two façades, with a tendency towards Baroque on this occasion, rather than to the Gothic style as in other works by the architect. The furniture, designed by Gaudí, is a very important aspect of Casa Calvet. On the ground floor it is made of oak, while on the first floor the furniture is upholstered. The furnishings are adorned with motifs inspired by the world of Nature.

The building known as Casa Batlló is

Part of the interior of the Palace.

Plaza de San Marcelo with the Casa de los Botines in the background.

another very characteristic example of Gaudí's civil architecture.

This house is situated in the Paseo de Gracia, Barcelona, next to Casa Amatller, which was designed by Puig i Cadafalch. Gaudí rebuilt the original edifice for the Batlló family, wealthy textile manufacturers. He began the work in 1904 and finished it two years later.

This was an optimal period of creativity for Gaudí. His original style had now triumphed and he was recognised as an architect of genius, attaining a degree of popularity without contemporary parallel.

His creative powers are evident not only in the architectural work involved in rebuilding Casa Batlló, but also in the design of the furniture. The furnishings of the dining-room will endure as an important example of Gaudí's sculptural sensitivity. As this room no longer exists in Casa Batlló, the furniture now forms part of the collections of the Gaudí House/Museum in Park Güell.

The glazed ceramics in blue tones covering the interior walls of Casa Batlló and the superb stair-well are very interesting, as also what remains of the furniture that Gaudí designed for the first floor.

The attic and terrace merit special mention, the architect designed them as an entirely new addition to the old building and they display original decoration. The visitor's attention is emphatically drawn to the dragon whose robust spine of scales stretches between a turret and a five-branched cross, on the façade giving onto the Paseo de Gracia. The enclosed balcony on the first floor is in Gaudí's purest style, of great plastic beauty.

Door and detail of the Casa de los Botines.

A detail of the stained glass windows of "Bellesguard".

Part of the staircase.

Casa Milá is arguably Gaudí's most successful, original secular design.
This unique building, popularly known as "la Pedrera" ("the Quarry"), is located on the Paseo de Gracia and was built by Gaudí between 1906 and 1910. This is in fact one of his most successful works. Salvador Tarragó, the architect, wrote that "La Pedrera represents the sculptural and architectural manifestation of his conception of Nature. Collins defined it as 'a mountain built by the

Facade of the Casa de Figueres or "Bellesguard". ▷

Mirror in the vestibule.

Lift and staircase to the floors. ▷

The rear facade of the Casa Calvet.

*Oak sofa and chair in the office on the
ground floor of the Casa Calvet.*

*Fragment of the sofa in the office on the
ground floor of the Casa Calvet.* ▷

hand of man.' Indeed, this colossal,
perforated cliff of architecture, with the
vast undulation of its façade resembling
a rough, immobile sea of stone — in
combination with 'the patina of the
stone, enriched by the flowers and clim-
bing plants on the balconies, which
would have given a constantly varied
colour to the building' (Gaudí's own
words) — constitutes the clearest ex-
pression of the Romantic, anti-classical
desire to naturalize architecture.''
La Pedrera is considered to be the most
original building of all the civil architecture in Barcelona, and is an indispen-
sable place to visit for foreign tourists
arriving in the city. Its interest resides
not only in the façade, but also in the
rooms inside and the patios.

Facade of the Casa Batlló.

Attic corridor and stairwell in the Casa Batlló.

Staircase to the main floor. ▷

Detail of the dragon's back and the scales on the Passeig de Gràcia side of the facade, with the tower and five-armed cross.

Fireplace on the main floor and part of the interior of the Casa Batlló.

The main flight of steps of the Parc Güell.

Sculptural detail of a central element of the main flight of steps. ▷

Park Güell constitutes one of the most fascinating exemplars of Gaudí's architectural originality.

This park is one of his most important, popular works; he began it in 1900 and finished in 1914. Don Eusebio Güell had commissioned it as a projected garden city for sixty houses. Park Güell stands on the site of the Can Montaner de Dalt property (Montaña Pelada — "Bare Mountain").

The enclosing wall, two entrance lodges and a large stairway were built; as also a temple in the Doric style supporting a large open space above, and the arches of the embankments for the road leading to the Park.

There are only two houses in the Park. One of them is now the Gaudí Museum, designed by Francisco Berenguer, which was Gaudí's home from 1906 to the year he died.

In the words of Salvador Tarragó, "In creating Park Güell, Gaudí achieved the only really new model of town-planning in the modernist period. To this end he separated the traffic of vehicles and pedestrians, allocating different routes to each. For pedestrians there were stairways and paths steeper than the internal road for carriages and cars, which had a maximum gradient of 1 in 15. Sometimes both routes were superimposed in such a way that the ramps

Main gate of the Parc Güell.

Detail of the roof of the porter's lodge. The prefabricated vertical elements act as a railing, whilst the topmost lantern is a chimney.

Lower colonnade of the Parc Güell.

above acted as roadways for vehicles and, being built on columns, they were used as covered arcades protecting pedestrians from the sun and rain for part of the way to the building plots.'' While Gaudí's work on Park Güell constituted a great achievement architecturally, from the financial point of view it was a failure, for of the sixty plots intended as sites for houses, only two were sold. Park Güell was a private garden until the 1920s, when Don Eusebio Güell's descendants ceded it to Barcelona *Ayuntamiento* (City Hall) to be converted into a public park.
Reinforced concrete was used for the first time in Spain in the construction of this great work by Gaudí. The famous undulating bench along the edge of the open space is extraordinarily beautiful: it was made of multicoloured tiles covering the walled-up prefabricated vaults used in its construction.
Gaudí worked in collaboration with his pupil José María Jujol, the architect, on the design of the vaults in the colonnade below, as also on the facing of the bench in the square; Jujol created the beautiful collages of glass, bottles and scraps of ceramics that foreshadowed abstract and surrealist works of art by several years.

View of the Parc
Güell from the
air with the
dragon on the
central flight
of steps.

Park Güell: the eye-catching bench; tower of the lodge on the left of the entrance.

Fragments of a bench in the Parc Güell. ▷

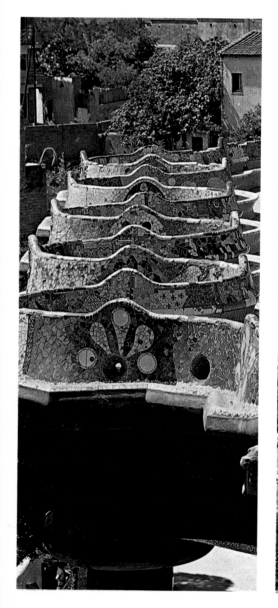

Decorative ceiling —by J. Jujol—
suspended beneath the square.

*Lower walk-viaduct. The vaults are
bricks covered with stone.*

Although it is not one of Gaudí's best-known works, the Sagrada Familia School is extremely interesting.
This building took him a year (1909-10); he built simple curved partition walls and an undulating roof, using bricks of considerable thickness. Le Corbusier was full of admiration for this little masterpiece when he saw it in 1928, and drew the inspiration for certain of his later designs from it.
Gaudí designed the handsome lamp-posts in the Plaza Real at the beginning of his professional career.

Staircase of the church of the Colonia Güell.

A facet of the interior of the church crypt.

Barcelona's civil authorities commissioned these cast-iron lampposts from him in 1878, to be installed in the Plaza Real, next to the Ramblas. This square was built by Daniel Francisco Molina Casamajó, on the site of the former Capuchin monastery.

While Gaudí was still a student of architecture, he designed for the Parque de la Ciudadela (under instructions from José Fontseré Mestres) various details of the "Monumental Waterfall" and of the balustrade around the monument to Aribau.

View of the Casa Milà from the air.

Balconies on the main facade of La Pedrera.

Gaudí's designs for the Colonia Güell are an outstanding feature of his architectural oeuvre.

Count Güell had a textile mill built in Santa Coloma de Cervelló, and beside it, a workers' housing estate, which was apparently designed by Gaudí's colleague Francisco Berenguer. Gaudí himself was the architect of the church, which was begun in 1898 and left unfinished in 1915; it stands at the foot of a small hillock, surrounded by woodland.

The estate's church displays vaults with brick partitions. "But," noted S. Tarragó, "their application is not restricted to the traditional use of these elastic structures, but rather he developed their possibilities to an unbelievable extent, going so far as to invent new applications, such as these exaggerated paraboloids. The crypt thus constitutes a complete inventory of all the structures that it is feasible to achieve by the use of bricks."

In the design of this masterpiece Gaudí succeeded in transcending the architectural parameters of the Gothic style, providing a new structural solution that opened the way to modes previously unknown in the field of architecture.

The universal admiration aroused by Gaudí and his oeuvre grows incessantly with the passage of time.

Chimneys and
doors to the flat
roof of the
Casa Milà.

View of the interior
of the courtyard in
the Carrer Provença.

Chimneys on the
flat roof of the
Casa Milà. ▷

Protegemos el bosque; papel procedente de cultivos forestales controlados
Wir schützen den Wald. Papier aus kontrollierten Forsten.
We protect our forests. The paper used comes from controlled forestry plantations
Nous sauvegardons la forêt: papier provenant de cultures forestières controlées

The printing of this book was completed
in the workshops of
FISA - ESCUDO DE ORO, S.A.
Palaudarias, 26 - Barcelona (Spain)